President Trump and My Neighbor

Please Allow Me to Introduce Myself
I'm a Man of Wealth and Shame
A Story of Two Different People Who Are Very Much the Same

MAX FOSTER

ISBN: 978-1-967361-65-6 (sc)
ISBN: 978-1-967361-66-3 (e)

Rev. date: 05/29/2025

Contents

I

Searching for a Place to Call Home

Once upon a time, about fifty years ago, people waved at each other in passing and said, "Good morning." They treated each other with respect. I know there was the occasional weird neighbor, but most of the time, everyone got along. It did not matter what political party you supported. You could count on your neighbor to help you if you needed help. Everyone was more willing to trust each other and enjoy the company of their neighbor.

The thing I miss the most is having a few beers and throwing horseshoes with my brothers and neighbors in the backyard while grilling something on the pit. You can pretty much say everything is opposite from the way it was once upon a time, fifty years ago.

We have heard the stories about the Black person knocking at the front door of a White homeowner, not realizing they were at the wrong address and getting shot because that homeowner feared for his life. I recall watching the news coverage of the parent going into his neighbors' backyard to retrieve a ball belonging to his son and getting shot for trespassing. The homeowner claimed to be "standing their ground," or whatever the hell they call it.

There is no need to continue with examples of how messed up things are. I think we all have a good idea of what has happened and what caused it to be this way. I have decided to do everything I can to communicate better or more effectively in the future.

*****

At the age of forty-two, I was a little terrified about becoming an old single dude. My first wife and I parted ways in 1990. The passing of time does seem to help clarify what happened when our relationship was falling apart. I will not bore anyone with the details, but I will say the stressful situation lasted five years.

For the first year of my single-dude status, I sat in my apartment, trying to figure out what the heck happened. They say it is good to have some kind of a pet to help get you through that difficult time. I did not even have a fish to talk to. Eventually, I got out of the apartment and started to enjoy myself instead of overthinking what might have caused the divorce. I finally remembered that old phrase: "You can't change what has happened in the past, but you do have control over what happens to you in the future."

I still enjoyed listening to my favorite music. I started to feel much better. I realized I could still laugh and enjoy the company of other people. I worked up enough courage to put on a pair of boots and my favorite pair of jeans so I could make an appearance at a place I used to go to when I was younger. We would socialize over a few beers, do some dancing, and enjoy the company of friends. I made sure there was no "looking for love in all the wrong places." I was not ready for that.

After socializing for a few weeks, I ran into a friend I had not seen in a long time. His name is Lee, and he told me about a fun group of people he was going to meet at the lake for a camping party. My first thought was *I don't know these people.* My second thought was *sounds like fun* because I do like meeting people and talking to them. Lee told me the people I met at the lake were from a singles group he hangs out with from a church. I thought, *How nice—a church group. I don't care for political groups or church groups.*

Lee invited me to go to the church he attended to learn more about these church folks. I reluctantly accepted his invitation and was glad I did. I believe I felt comfortable meeting more of his friends because I had already camped out with some of them at the lake.

The church is a very large popular church in Austin, Texas. They have singles groups for all ages—teens to seniors. Each group had their calendar of events and fun things to do every week. They allowed you to be whoever you wanted to be. They did not try to force you into believing or worshiping in a certain way. They realize everyone is different, and that's the way it should be. I agree totally with that concept. We all have the right to think and believe what we want to believe, feel how we want to feel, and do whatever we want to do—as long as we don't break the law or harm other people. Anyway, I enjoyed visiting this very large popular church.

One Sunday, when the group was meeting to discuss some of the events they had planned, I noticed a very attractive lady at the front of the group. She almost knocked me out of my Sunday school chair. She was going over what was on the calendar. I sat up in my chair and paid attention to every word she said. She was soft-spoken, kind, and very attractive. No, it was not too soon to be noticing a woman in that way. Would I be going to this church if there were no attractive women in this group of single adults? Probably not. Six years had passed since I divorced my first wife. All I remember thinking was *Here I am in church being introduced to an angel.* Kind of cool, right?

Shelly and I had lots of friends and enjoyed various activities with the group of singles. We danced, went horseback riding on the beach, played at a large waterpark, and then danced again. These people were good, honest, kind people. This was also the time when Shelly and I got to know each other. We did have a great courtship. I trusted her, and she felt the same way about me—no issues like past relationship problems, jealousy, insecurity, or any of that junk. All my exes live in Texas, but none of them bothered us.

About six months after we met, I asked Shelly to marry me, and she said, "Oh, hell yes." She didn't really respond that way, but she did give me the answer I wanted. A couple of months after that, we promised to love, honor, and be kind to each other for as long as we both shall live.

*****

Shelly had gotten an offer to teach at a college in Wyoming. I think we were both excited about traveling to Wyoming and living where the buffalo roam. Shelly made lots of friends at the school where she worked, and I got me a job driving a school bus. Some of my friends were first and second and third graders. I was not able to continue working for the postal service because Sheriden is a small town, and the only people working there are friends and relatives of the postmaster.

The powers to be had offered to give Shelly an increase in her wages after her first year of teaching. She did not get an increase. Instead, they informed her there would be a decrease in pay. She had worked hard and did a really good job during her first year of teaching. I was pissed about what they did, so we loaded up the truck and moved to Beverly—I mean Idaho.

We purchased a nice split-level home with a large backyard in Post Falls, Idaho. Shelly did like teaching, but she decided to work as a dental hygienist for a while.

I don't remember how long it took before she was diagnosed with fibromyalgia, but she was no longer able to work as a hygienist. She could not hold onto her instruments, and eventually, the pain reached a point where she could not function at all. Shelly had to stop working in 1998. Our income had been reduced by 50 percent. She was very upset about what was happening to her. No one wants to be totally derailed like she was.

We stayed in the home in Post Falls as long as we could. It was time to downsize and find a more affordable home to live in. We eventually found five acres of land with a single wide manufactured home on it thirty miles north of Spokane, Washington. It was just what we were looking for. I did not want to live in a single wide trailer house, but there was a large pole barn/garage we could store all the things that would not fit in the skinny house until we could have a larger home placed on the property. It was a great piece of land with lots of potential. This was the best address we have ever had in regard to how it sounded. The words *Whitetail* and *Elk* are in the address. It did, however, turn out to be the worst address I have ever had.

There was a large red flag flapping in the wind in front of the Coeur d' Alene Idaho Resort on Sherman Avenue. The flag had a black cross in the middle with a white background. Shelly and I could not believe we were witnessing the starting point of what was a KKK march through downtown Coeur d' Alene. These people were in uniform—white sheets with a pointed hood and swastikas. Guess that was why we did not see any people of color when we moved to Idaho. We should have paid attention to this very large red flag. It turned out to be the same behavior we witnessed in Eastern Washington. Washington is a blue state, but the east side is very red. I will talk more about this type of behavior later in the story.

We adjusted financially, but we soon realized we were living in an area with several neighbors from hell. It was as if we had landed in the middle of a cult. The people in this area were very antisocial, antigovernment, antineighbor, and antieverything. It was the strangest thing Shelly and I had ever experienced.

None of the neighbors would wave at you. There were no invitations to play backyard games or indoor card games.

I was waiting for one of the neighbors to show up with a plate of cookies to welcome us to the neighborhood, but it never happened. Instead of cookies, we were introduced to the area with an insanely loud mud-racing truck by our closest neighbor. Yes, we could have gone back to the real estate company and demanded our money back so we could keep looking for a better place; but at this point, I decided I am getting too old for all this moving, so we just decided to see how things played out.

The most interesting of the new neighbors from hell is a spoiled-rotten only child of parents living in a nice golf-course community about ten miles southwest of our property. Most of the people living in the nice community own nice vehicles, nice homes, and nice other stuff. It's all very nice. I think I will call the spoiled-rotten child from hell Adolf. (I might also refer to him as SROC.) Not long after we moved into this home, the spoiled-rotten child started revving and working on the (extremely loud) mud-racing truck.

The mud racer was a pickup truck with a big block engine, no muffler, and very large tires. It was designed to race through an area of mud about three hundred feet long. It was extremely loud. Everyone would get muddy and drink lots of beer. I can think of a number of ways to go out and have fun, but this sure as hell would not be one of them. I think the mud racing must have taken place in the next county.

Mud-Racing Truck

The noise was so loud we could not have a conversation with anyone on the phone. We could not hear the TV or each other. I am pretty sure the walls were shaking.

We had two potbellied pigs at the time. When Adolf would race the engine of the mud-racing truck, the pigs would run around in circles, trying to get away from the noise. I felt sorry for them and the horse Dipstick owned. This went on for the next four years.

Adolf would work on the truck during the week, tuning it up and getting it ready for the race on the weekend. We did retain a lawyer, but all he could do is type up a cease-and-desist order. Mr. Adolf did receive the order in the mail, but the very next summer, he was back to making all sorts of noise to harass and intimidate us. His goal was to run us off our property. There are residential homes in this area.

It is crazy to think someone could make this kind of noise next door to my house. I did ask my neighbor if he could work on his truck in a different location. He said he was doing that, but he could no longer work on it where he was, so he had to work on it at his home.

I felt like asking him what planet he was from because the people on this planet know it is not cool to do that in an area zoned rural tradition. Things got even more exciting when Adolf started driving a loud dirt bike all around the neighborhood to make more noise. His kids would drive an ATV up and down the private road we live on.

The kids on the ATV were not that noisy, but they did create lots of dust in front of our house. I remember watching the dad get on the ATV and drive it at top speed down the dusty private road. When he stopped, he would drive the ATV at full throttle in a tight circle in order to create as much dust as possible, thinking it would blow in the direction of our home. On that day, the wind was blowing in the direction of his house, and he had to take in most of the dust he created himself. It was fun to watch this angry adult child attempt to do something he thought would bother me.

II

Several Neighbors from Hell

Adolf is also a mechanic, and he does work for an electric company in Spokane. He drives the large bucket trucks from a location in Spokane, Washington, to his home next to our house to work on them.

The other neighbor from hell moved into the house across the road from us about three years after we moved into our home. One day, he showed up while I was working in my yard. He introduced himself and started asking political questions. I told him how I felt and what I believed should have been done about the 9/11 attack on our country. I don't think he liked what I had to say.

I said the people from Iraq did not attack our country; the son of a Saudi prince by the name of Osama bin Laden and a group of his friends are the people who attacked our country and killed over three thousand of our people. I also said I thought Barack Obama was way smarter than George W. Bush. In their minds (Adolf and Vladimir), you don't have the right to think or say whatever you want to say. It was at this time both of the neighbors from hell decided to run us off our property. They used an insanely loud mud-racing truck, ATVs, dirt bikes, loud revving of hot rods, constant loud shooting, and whatever else they could think of to "run us off."

The harassment has lasted over eighteen years so far.

*****

Shelly and I realized at this point in our lives we were experiencing something we had never seen before. We got no help from the sheriff's department, no help from county code enforcement, and no help from anyone else. Washington State is a blue state, but the east side is very red. If you take into consideration how our country has become so politically divided, you will understand what I mean. We have recently elected a Democrat to replace the Republican mayor of Spokane, which was followed by replacing the sheriff as well as several other positions held by Republicans.

It is interesting how similar local politics is to national politics these days. The county codes and noise disturbance ordinances are designed to protect the homeowners (all of the homeowners, not just the affluent ones). It is also interesting how similar Donald Trump's sociopathic behavior is to my neighbors'.

I do not share the same political views as my neighbors, so I guess I do not belong in their neighborhood. I forgot to mention things have gotten better since the changes in leadership here in the east side of Washington State.

I will say—if I haven't already—we have never done anything to cause these two people to think it is necessary or okay to treat us the way they have for a very long time. We also have never seen people act the way they do in this neighborhood or area. It is fascinating to witness this kind of behavior for such a long time.

In addition to being fascinating, it is also frustrating, stressful, annoying, and sad. I use the word *fascinating* because these people have built a wall between themselves and others who do not agree with them on issues and politics. They think it is not possible to enjoy the company of others who are different than them. It is possible to agree to disagree. You can feel the way you want to feel, and I can do the same. I used the word *sad* because they are teaching their children how to be disrespectful to seniors and veterans.

The neighbor living across the private road from us created a dirt bike track around his house for his son and his friends. The dirt bikes are very loud, and it is like having motocross races all the time across the road from your house. Adolf and Vladimir shoot a variety of loud weapons for hours at a time. They call it target practicing. The only difference between the KKK march in Idaho during the late nineties and the KKK soldiers of today is the ones today wear camo with their faces covered, and they carry assault weapons.

The neighbor from hell closest to us plays his music as loud as he can for hours at a time every weekend. The noise disturbance ordinance clearly states all of the different types of noises I have mentioned are prohibited.

*****

One of the most disturbing things about all this disrespectful behavior is the parents of these children do all these things in front of their children and then wonder why they get in trouble on the school bus and in school. All of the older people, except for me, wonder, *What the hell is wrong with these kids?* Now that I have studied these people, I would like to leave. Just kidding; I wanted to leave eighteen years ago, but we have had lots of pets during the time we have lived at this address; and in most cases, we could not take them with us if we moved, and it is hard to find new owners that you would want to leave these pets with especially in this area.

Shelly and I do believe our pets and working hard to make improvements on the property are what helped us get through years of whatever Adolf and Vlad wanted to dish out. I did feel like pounding both of the neighbors from hell into the ground, but I realized I would be the one put in jail, not them. Our judicial system is also kind of messed up these days. I also realized the sheriff's office would not do anything to help with the constant loud noise, so I purchased a good set of noise-canceling earbuds so I could listen to my favorite music while working. I was determined to "stand my ground." I know that term is supposed to mean something else, but it works in my case also. It is important to be who you want to be, think whatever you want to think, and feel how you want to feel.

THE WHIPPLE LAW GROUP PLLC, Leading with Legal Solutions

905 W. Riverside Ave.
Suite 408
Spokane, WA 99201

May 29, 2014

David Corder
41130 N. Whitetail Ln.
Elk, WA 99009

RE: *Demand to Cease and Desist*

Dear Mr. Corder:

We represent your neighbors David and Shannon Linder. You and our clients both live in a quiet, rural residential neighborhood where the homeowners have the right to the quiet enjoyment of their property. Your behavior, as a neighbor in this community, is egregious and has caused our clients considerable distress and hardship. These actions include unlawful auto salvage, commercial vehicle repair operations, consistent and repeated violation of maximum permissible noise levels, trespass of your animals, personal threats, and verbal abuse. The intolerable conditions created by your actions constitute a nuisance and continue to directly interfere with your neighbors' reasonable enjoyment and use of their property.

Our clients' repeated attempts to reach a cordial accommodation with you have been met with nothing but unreasoning anger, obstinacy, and threats. As you are aware, your persistent pattern of actions violates several municipal ordinances and Washington statutory law. *See e.g.* RCW 7.48.120, 260; SCC 6.12.010; 040; 6.13.010 *et. seq.*, WAC 173-60, 62. There is a long history of police and code enforcements reports and additional evidence documenting your persistent illegal actions.

Our clients' patience is at an end. You should consider this communication and our intentions with the utmost seriousness.

If you do not immediately and permanently desist from the described actions, as well as any additional nuisance type conduct entirely, our clients are prepared to take prompt legal action to seek redress including damages for the injuries they have incurred.

In addition, we hereby put you on notice that any further retaliatory actions against our client will not be tolerated. Please inform us if you are legally represented and direct any responding correspondence to our offices.

Sincerely,

Michael D. Whipple
Attorney at Law

Everything was starting to look good. We also had over fifty trees removed to reduce the possibility of losing our home in a wildfire. Later we had a new manufactured home moved onto our property, and we had our little rail fence by the road painted.

The flower beds looked good, and the front and backyard were green and groomed. The new manufactured home we had moved onto the property looked very nice. I also purchased two out-buildings for what would be the homes for the potbellied pigs we have had over the years.

We also had a water well drilled and installed on our property. We were sharing a well with Adolf, Vlad, and one other extremist in the area. Adolf had threatened to shut off our water because the well that we shared was on his property. He was a fool for making such a threat. Shelly and I felt this might be the last thing we needed to do before putting a FOR SALE sign up. The well-drilling company had to go down to 530 feet to find a water source. There seems to be plenty of water for watering the lawn, showering, doing the laundry, etc. I will include photos of our home and property. You might see an occasional dog, pig, or cat running around; they help to improve the look of our property also.

Chapter 6.12 - NOISE DISTURBANCES

Sections:

6.12.010 - Noise disturbances prohibited.

(a) It is unlawful for any person to make, continue, cause to be made, or to allow to originate from real property in the possession of said person, any sound which creates a noise disturbance.

(b) For the purposes of this section, the following sounds are declared to be noise disturbances:

   (1) Sounds created by use of a radio, television set, musical instrument, sound amplifier or any other device capable of producing or reproducing sound, which emanate frequently, repetitively or continuously from any building, structure or property located within a residential area, and which annoy or disturb the peace, comfort or repose of a reasonable person of normal sensitivity;

   (2) Any other sound occurring frequently, repetitively or continuously which annoys or disturbs the peace, comfort or repose of a reasonable person of normal sensitivity. This section shall not apply to noncommercial public speaking and public assembly activities conducted on any public space or public right-of-way for which a permit has been obtained. Additionally, this section shall not apply to noises governed by Spokane County Code Chapter 5.04 (Dog control ordinance).

(Res. 90-0667 Attachment A (part), 1990: Res. 90-0638 Attachment B (part), 1990)

6.12.020 - Exemptions.

(a) The following shall be exempt from the provisions of Section 6.12.010:

   (1) Sounds created by motor vehicles when regulated by WAC Chapter 173-62;

   (2) Sounds originating from aircraft in flight and sounds that originate at airports which are directly related to flight operations;

   (3) Sounds created by surface carrier engaged in commerce or passenger travel by railroad;

   (4) Sounds created by warning devices not operating continuously for more than five minutes, or bells, chimes or carillons;

   (5) Sounds created by safety and protective devices where noise suppression would defeat the intent of the device or is not economically feasible;

   (6) Sounds created by emergency equipment and work necessary in the interest of law enforcement or for health, safety or welfare of the community;

   (7) Sounds originating from motor vehicle racing events at existing authorized facilities;

   (8) Sounds originating from officially sanctioned parades and other public events;

   (9) Sounds emitting from petroleum refinery boilers during startup of the boilers; provided, that the startup operation is performed during daytime hours whenever possible;

   (10) Sounds created by watercraft, except to the extent that they are regulated by other county ordinances;

   (11) Sounds created by the discharge of firearms in the course of hunting;

   (12) Sounds created by motor vehicles licensed or unlicensed when operated off public highways, except when such sounds are made in or adjacent to residential property where human beings reside or sleep;

   (13) Sounds originating from existing natural gas transmission and distribution facilities;

   (14) Sounds created in conjunction with public work projects or public work maintenance operations executed at the cost of the federal government, state or municipality;

(15) Sounds created in conjunction with the collection of solid wastes;

(16) Sounds created in conjunction with military operations or training;

(17) Sounds originating from organized activities occurring in public parks, playgrounds, gymnasiums, swimming pools, and other public recreational facilities during hours of operation;

(18) Sounds originating from agricultural activities.

(b) The following shall be exempt from the provisions of Section 6.12.010 between the hours of seven a.m. and ten p.m.:

    (1) Sounds originating from residential property relating to temporary projects for the repair or maintenance of homes, grounds and appurtenances;

    (2) Sounds created by the discharge of firearms on authorized shooting ranges;

    (3) Sounds created by blasting;

    (4) Sounds created by aircraft engine testing and maintenance not related to flight operations; provided, that aircraft testing and maintenance shall be conducted at remote sites whenever possible;

    (5) Sounds created by the installation or repair of essential utility services.

(c) The following shall be exempt from the provisions of Section 6.12.010 between the hours of seven a.m. and ten p.m., or when conducted beyond one thousand feet of any residence where human beings reside and sleep at any hour:

    (1) Sounds originating from temporary construction sites as a result of construction activity;

    (2) Sounds originating from forest harvesting and silvicultural activity;

    (3) Sounds originating from the quarrying, blasting and mining of minerals or materials, including, but not limited to, sand, gravel, rock and clay, as well as the primary reduction and processing of minerals or materials for concrete batching, asphalt mixing and rock crushers;

    (4) Sounds originating from uses on properties which have been specifically conditioned to meet certain noise standards by an appropriate Spokane County hearing body.

(Res. 90-0667 Attachment A (part), 1990: Res. 90-0638 Attachment B (part), 1990)

6.12.030 - Violation—Misdemeanor—Penalty.

Any person violating any of the provisions of this chapter shall be deemed guilty of a misdemeanor, and upon conviction thereof, shall be punished by imprisonment in the Spokane County Jail for a period of not more than ninety days, or by a fine of not more than one thousand dollars, or by both such imprisonment and fine.

(Res. 90-0667 Attachment A (part), 1990: Res. 90-0638 Attachment B (part), 1990)

6.12.040 - Violation—Civil infraction—Penalty.

(a) In addition to, or as an alternative to, those provisions set forth in Section 6.12.030, a violation of any of the provisions of this chapter shall constitute a civil infraction, subject to a monetary penalty in the amount of fifty dollars per day for each violation. Each such violation shall be a separate and distinct offense, and in case of a continuing violation, each day's continuance shall be a separate and distinct violation.

(b) The procedures for issuance of a notice of infraction, hearings, assessment and payment of monetary penalties shall be in accordance with the provisions of RCW Chapter 7.80. Hearings on notices of infractions issued pursuant to this section shall be held in the Spokane County District Court.

(Res. 90-0667 Attachment A (part), 1990: Res. 90-0638 Attachment B (part), 1990)

6.12.050 - Severability.

If any provision of this chapter is held invalid or unconstitutional, the remainder of the chapter shall not be affected thereby.

III

Please Allow Me to Introduce Myself

I like to refer to Donald Trump as a male slut. When his campaign was just getting started, he was kind of in trouble for being involved with a porn star by the name of Stormy Daniels. He, of course, denied anything happened between him and Daniels. I think this was one of the many lies I have heard him tell. Some people think it is okay to lie about something; it just means they were raised differently than you were.

When I thought things could not get worse, along came the Trump campaign. Some people were very impressed with his style. Others could not believe what they were hearing and seeing. Personally, I was in a state of disappointment, disbelief, discussed, and some other *dis* words. There are several things I find very disturbing about this orange, chubby guy that thinks he is really smart. I learned from the first two years of his term he is also a very dangerous man. We are starting to see why the Trump cult is so strong. I believe he could make the majority of his followers drink some purple Kool-Aid. Candidate Trump had an unusual way of communicating with his fellow Republicans and even other people who opposed him.

He also made racist remarks, had no respect for women, and totally screwed up the way the pandemic should have been handled. I would say too many people died because Trump would say it's kind of like the flu; it will go away in a couple of weeks. He would not even acknowledge global warming and probably still does not. I do believe he is the most unqualified person for the job of the president of this country. If he does get elected, he will be a great dictator.

President Trump and lots of other people do not read about the history of this country. If they did, they would not say things like churches should be able to express political views during services without losing their tax-exempt status. There is this thing called separation between church and state.

The president sort of accidentally shared highly classified information with the Russians. He also shared classified information with his *Fox News* friends every morning instead of consulting with his staff or congress before making those big decisions. A good example would be when he had the second in command of the Iranian military killed by way of a drone strike without notifying anyone first—very, very dangerous.

Here is a good example of something or someone getting way too powerful. The NRA has control over politicians, street gangs, and all the Trump supporters that love to hate and think they need an assault weapon to protect their families. Just look around. How many people have died by the hand of a gunman lately? I will never have as much power as the NRA or the Republicans, but I will always have the right to say whatever I want to say about gun violence or bump stocks.

IV

A Test of Strength and Patience

When Adolf realized I did not like the idea of him making so much noise, he started driving a loud ATV with no muffler up and down the private road we live on. This is the kind of behavior you would expect to see with a person that suddenly pops up straight out of hell or a spoiled-rotten only child.

The reason I bring up the fact that he must be from hell is because two years after we moved into the house next door to the "devil," I heard someone yelling very loudly at another person. He was swearing at him and calling him all sorts of names. My first thought was I would never talk to or yell at anyone like that. About two weeks later, I was told the person this neighbor from hell was yelling at was his father. They were building a covered deck onto the back of the house his father was letting him and his family live in. My second thought was if my son talked to me or yelled at me like that, it would be the last time he treated me with that kind of disrespect.

You would think that much noise and very bad behavior would be enough, but it was not for Adolf. He would also drive the ATV at full throttle up and down the private road.

*****

At this point, I was trying to figure out why Adolf seemed to be totally consumed with trying to harass me and Shelly. He spent a lot of his time shooting guns, driving a very loud ATV, dirt bike, hot rod he had built in his garage in the neighborhood.

Adolf also had a red dirt bike that was—you guessed it—very loud. He would drive the dirt bike all around the neighborhood and up and down the private road. The ATV, dirt bike, and hot rod noise would occur several times a day almost every day. I guess the best way to describe him is to say he is a narcissistic, disrespectful racist and a spoiled-rotten adult boy. (Wow, it is hard to do that without using bad language.)

I do use an occasional bad word, but I attribute that to my difficulty with learning how to read and not knowing many big words.

One day, Shelly returned from a trip to town, and she told me something odd happened when she stopped at the convenience store on the way home. The store had a car wash and an area you can use to vacuum and clean up your car. When Shelly was cleaning her car outside the store, suddenly there was a very loud noise coming from a car parked at the gas pumps. The loud noise was similar to the loud revving of the mud-racing vehicle, the dirt bikes, and ATVs my evil neighbors have used to harass us and try to run us off our property. Who would have thought Dipstick would take his unacceptable behavior out into the public? The public harassment lasted for approximately twenty minutes.

After revving the car by the gas pumps for a while, he pulled up behind Shelly's car and continued his public intimidation. Shelly said the other customers in the area started yelling at him, saying, "What is your problem?" I think Shelly did not call 911 to ask for help because she knew it would take them too long to get there, and she was just hoping Dipstick would get tired of what he was doing and go away.

The next day, I drove to the Spokane County Courthouse to inquire about the zoning in the area we lived in. It is rural traditional, not commercial. Mr. Pain-in-the-Butt is a mechanic, and he works on commercial trucks for a company named Power City Electric in his garage and driveway. He did maintenance and repair work on the trucks and the occasional knocking out of dents, sanding, and painting of large trucks, which is a county code violation. There is also a Spokane County noise disturbance ordinance that is totally ignored by my neighbors and the Spokane County Sheriff's Department.

Instead of getting angry about the insane amount of noise, I decided to get a job driving a school bus for the school district. Maybe replacing the adult child next door with some real children would be a good idea. I replaced the feeling of anger with something positive like driving a bus full of sweet little schoolchildren to school instead of constantly thinking about living next to the devil and his buddy.

*****

I started to realize the county officials such as the code enforcement office, the sheriff's office, and the mayor should start to do their jobs. You are going to see people that seem to love breaking the law, but you should be able to count on county officials to enforce the laws.

I was really enjoying interacting with the kids, and it was fun talking to them. I especially enjoyed the kindergarten, first and second graders. They were the sweet uncorrupted ones that were well behaved.

Halfway through the school year, a third grader started

swearing and acting bad on the bus, so I wrote her up for her behavior. A few days later, I was talking with one of the other bus drivers, and she told me she had to write up one of the girls on her bus for the same reason. The girl on the other bus was my neighbor's daughter, who thought it was okay to use really bad language because her father did while working on trucks in his garage and in his driveway.

A few days later, my neighbor (Adolf) came over to my house and knocked on our front door. When I answered the door, I could see my neighbor was upset about something, so I asked him, "What's up?"

He said he was pissed because I was talking trash behind his back.

I said, "Could you be more specific?"

He went on to say I should not have said what I said to the other bus driver. He also described the kids getting into trouble on the bus for using bad language on the bus.

My response was "So what part of what I said was not true?"

He started mumbling and backing up off my porch as I was stepping closer to his face.

As he was walking back to his house, he was threatening to kick my ass. Later I asked him why he was using really loud bad language in me. His response was he did it because he thought it would upset. He went on to tell me I should not have said what I said to the other bus driver.

My first year of school bus driving turned out to be a very bad experience. There was a third grader I had to write up for bad behavior on the bus. She had an older sister that was in the fifth or sixth grade. The third grader was angry because I had written her up, so one day, she pretended to be stuck between the seat and the finder well of the bus. I instructed her older sister to stay with her until we arrived at school. I had also called in the situation to the bus manager. When we got to the school, we got help from a lady who was there to help with any problems we might have. The third grader was fine, and all was well.

About a week later, I was accused of inappropriate touching of the third grader that seemed to have placed herself between the finder well and the seat of the bus. There was an investigation of the incident, and it was determined I had not acted inappropriately.

After I had time to think about what happened that day, I decided the third grader was angry about getting written up, so she went to her older sister, who coached her little sister on how to get the bus driver in trouble. I did not do anything wrong, but I had gotten dirty looks from some of the other drivers for the period of time it took to do the investigation—definitely one of the most embarrassing things that has ever happened to me.

Trucks from Work

Play the Hand You Are Dealt

In the year 2007, Shelly and I decided to start a pet sitting service. I am so glad we did because it helped take our minds off the crazy behavior of our neighbors from hell.

This would be my third way to "deal with the devil and lies." I do try hard not to get political when I am writing a story like this one. I will just say this divide did not exist until postelection 2020 followed by the insurrection.

At first, the petsitting business was a little slow; but after the first year, we were able to get lots of customers. I think one of the reasons was we would go to the customers' home to care for their pets. This way, the pets would not get as stressed because we were the ones traveling, not the pets. It was kind of like housesitting and petsitting together. The other reason was we had a veterinary clinic about six miles from our home, and we were a regular customer. They referred lots of people to our service.

After we had been in business for three years, we had more clients than we could handle, so we hired some helpers. It was kind of a challenge because at this point, we were doing more paperwork and less interacting with the pets. We hired six helpers to help with the increase in the number of clients we had.

We did background checks on each one of them before we hired them. Our clients knew they could trust us. They did not worry about their pets or their property when they were gone on vacation or whatever they wanted to do. The only mistake we made was not charging our customers enough for our service. Shelly and I both are animal lovers, and we really enjoyed spending time with the pets we cared for.

LEAVING TOWN? HAVE PETS WHY NOT CALL?

NEIGHBOR DAVE'S PETSITTING!

*Professional, loving pet care in your home.
* One, two or three visits offered daily.
* Mail brought in and plants watered.
* Theft deterrence while you are away.

* INSURED * BONDED * MEMBER OF PET SITTERS
INTERNATIONAL & PUPS

website: neighbordavespetsitting.com

I don't know how we did it, but we managed to keep up with all the yard work and projects around the house. I think we tried to stay as busy as possible to keep our minds off the crazy constant harassment.

This rather large boy's name is Reddy, one of the sweetest dogs on the planet. The Newfoundland breed is a special breed of dog. They are one of the gentlest, kindest dogs I have ever seen.

This is what I call Beegle madness. These are show dogs that spend the nights in a crate, and when they are taken out to get some fresh air, they go a little crazy.

This beautiful boy is Bob. Bob was a member of our family; he did not belong to one of our customers. He is, however, one of the best-looking dogs I have ever seen.

He was a very laid-back big love sponge. He was abused by his previous owner. We tried to work with him, but he was too broken. We had to have him euthanized after a few dog bites. They were not serious; it just made us realize he was a dangerous dog.

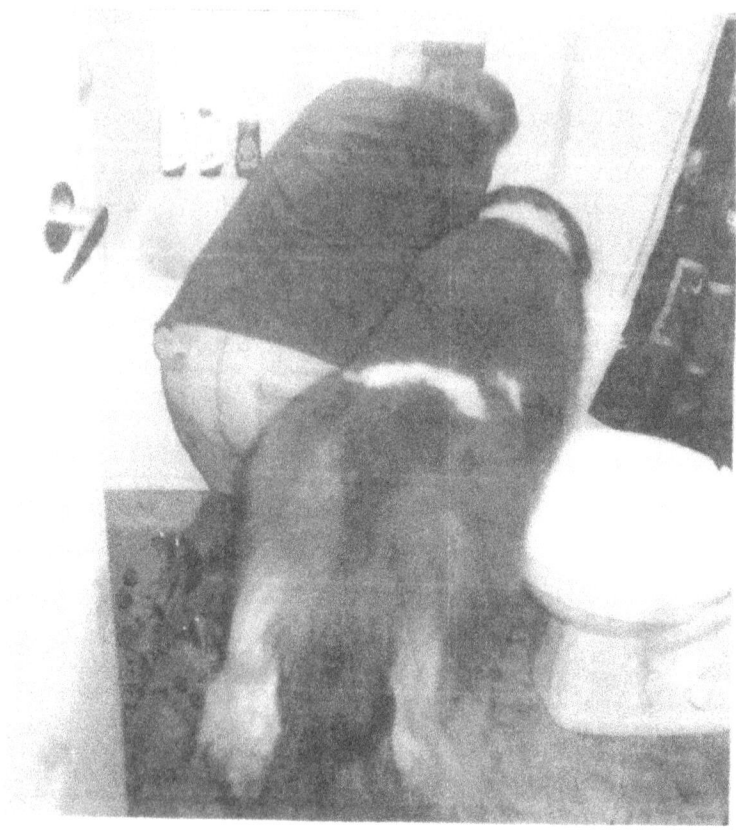

This is Berta; she is also a large dog. We adopted her because she was such a sweet, loving girl. She only did one bad thing when we had her, and I don't think she realized she was doing anything wrong. One day, Shelly had her in the backyard on a leash to keep her away from the potbellied pig. I think Berta did not want to be on a leash, so she ran down the back porch steps and across the backyard with Shelly holding onto the leash—a Funniest Home Video moment. She is helping me clean the bathtub. I'm not sure, but I think her butt is wider than mine?

VI

Don't Ever Give Up

At the beginning and all through this story, I would say, "I do not understand why the Spokane County Sheriff's Department and the County Code Enforcement Office would not help us with these very annoying neighbors." From this day forward, I am going to stop asking myself that question.

If I am going to be upset about something, it should be the fact that it took me so long to realize hate, lies, corruption, and disrespect are just as much—if not more—a problem in local and state governments as it is in national government.

I remember the day that light flashed in my head, and I realized what was really going on. I try very hard to be positive and thankful for what I have, but when you are harassed this much for such a long time for no reason, you start to wonder. Should I get some therapy for this condition I have? That might be a good thing to do. It helps a lot to talk with someone about how totally screwed up our country is today. We did not know this area was filled with people who love loud dirt bikes, loud ATVs, loud race cars, loud target shooting, and loud Trump worship. There was so much shooting I thought there was going to be another "Ruby Ridge" thing in this area.

Warning signs should say, "CAUTION: there is no law enforcement in this part of the county. No attempts will be made to enforce the laws or ordinances that are there to protect the homeowners." Go ahead, call me crazy.

*****

Why would anyone stay in an area like the one we had lived in for such a long time?

I guess I feel like my wife and I should be able to have a nice home on five acres of land and enjoy what's left of our lives. We also love having a garden, dogs, cats, potbellied pigs, and the sound of Canadian geese flying over all the time.

We still have too many pets to move to another area, and the cost of purchasing another home these days is a little scary. The cost of purchasing anything is crazy.

There is one other thing to consider. The two neighbors that have dished out all the insane harassment over the years seem to have matured enough to make life bearable. I still think they both are boys trapped in the bodies of an adult.

I recall saying to Shelly, "I would not have ever imagined in my wildest dreams this could happen to a couple who were Vietnam and Vietnam-era veterans and a retired postal employee who did not go postal on these idiots. If you are looking for a place to live and you see Proud Boy, Oath Keeper, and Trump flags flapping in the wind, keep looking for a place in the next county. I think owning five acers of land, adopting shelter animals, and starting a pet care business helped us get through these extremely stressful years. I wonder how many of us are left that believe in love, honesty, and kindness instead of lies and hate. It takes a little effort to be respectful.

*****

It is easier to say, "F—— off. I don't give a damn what you think." It's like if I don't agree with them about everything, talk like them, and walk like them, I don't belong in their world, which is also this neighborhood. They are right; I don't belong. I think it is healthy to disagree. It is even healthier to calmly discuss issues, listen, and respect others right to their opinion.

We are bombarded with negative junk on the news and social media every day. I would like to bombard you with good stuff. Do you have a favorite comedian, type of music, place to go, game to play, or anything that makes you feel good? Don't say you do not; I know you do. Hopefully you will give me a chance to tell you why.

There are people wondering what they can do to help change or improve the "hell" we are surrounded by in today's politically divided country. If-you-don't-agree-with-someone-punch-him-in-the-face kind of attitude? I know that there are people out there that feel the same way I do. We all do have the right to express our opinions, and there are lots of different ways to do it without insulting whoever we are communicating with.

RIP Big Guy

When we heard Bob was looking for a home, I thought, *Wow! This is the dog I have always wanted.* We adopted Bob from a family living in the same area.

After we had him for a couple of weeks, I could tell something was not right with him. When I tried to correct him, he would get aggressive. Three dog bites later, we decided it would be dangerous to keep him. The previous owner must have abused him.

GOODBYE EVERYONE

*President Trump Boarding Air Force One
with Toilet Paper Stuck to his shoe.*

www.ingramcontent.com/pod-product-compliance
Lightning Source LLC
Chambersburg PA
CBHW051249120626
46547CB00014B/1869